Beautiful America's
San Diego

Front cover: The skyline from Harbor Island

Published by
Beautiful America Publishing Company
P.O. Box 244
Woodburn, OR 97071

Library of Congress Catalog Number
92--42559

ISBN 0-89802-741-1
ISBN 0-89802--740-3 (paperback)

Printed in Korea

The Tower from Santa Fe Passenger Depot

Beautiful America's

San Diego

Photography by Ken Naversen

Text by Andrea Naversen

Beautiful America Publishing Company

Contents

Introduction

I'm a wanderer at heart, a vagabond. My brothers and I grew up all over the United States, as the children of an Air Force officer and his wife, parents who gave us a sense of security despite all those moves. One year here. Two years there. In big towns and little towns. The constant moving gave me a sense of independence–being the new kid on the block will do that–and a curiosity for what lay beyond my own backyard.

And so as a print journalist, and later as a television reporter, my wanderings continued. Three years here. Four years there. In big towns and little towns.

I'm still a wanderer at heart, but one now with roots firmly planted in San Diego. This, finally, is home. It's not just the weather that keeps me here, although warm, sunny days year-round do tend to spoil you. It's not just the blue Pacific breaking a few miles from my door. And it's not just the wealth of things to do, whether it's a day on the beach or a night at the Old Globe.

What keeps me here is San Diego's sense of community. It's a big town, but somehow it has managed to retain a small town feel. You know your neighbors here. You belong. San Diego is sort of like the bar in the old TV show, "Cheers." It's a warm, familiar place. Here, everybody knows your name. Or maybe it just feels that way.

The view from East Basin, San Diego Bay

Opposite: Skyline at sunset

San Diego

I thought San Diego must be a heaven on earth, if it was all as fine as that. It seemed to me the best spot for building a city I ever saw.

Alonzo Horton is still right after all these years. On April 15, 1867, he first set eyes on San Diego. And he liked what he saw–San Diego Bay, the peninsula that would later be called Coronado Island, the long spit of land known as Point Loma. The father of San Diego had found his heaven on earth.

But little did Horton know how important San Diego would become. It's now the seventh largest city in the United States. Most people think of San Diego as a tourist town, with miles of beaches, near perfect weather, and world famous attractions. But residents know it is so much more. Once considered just a sleepy little town by the bay, the city has come into its own. It has a strong economy, low crime and unemployment, cultural diversity, excellent health care, top universities, and–did we mention–*lots* of sun.

San Diego is also a military town. Major Navy and Marine facilities make this among the biggest military complexes in the United States. It's home to one of the largest and busiest naval ports in the world–many of the Pacific Fleet's carriers, cruisers, and submarines are stationed here. And jets based at Marine Corps Air Station Miramar soar through San Diego's skies.

It's also a science town. World famous research facilities located here include the Salk Institute, the Scripps Research Institute, and the Burnham Institute. San Diego is also home to a burgeoning high-tech/biotech industry. It has the third largest concentration of biotechnology companies in the nation. And it is fertile ground for the growth of high technology–from computer components to telecommunications, cell phones to high definition television. The Greater San Diego Chamber of Commerce boasts: "There are more PhDs, more personal computers and more fiber optic cable" in San Diego than anywhere else in the country.

San Diego is a sports town, as well. It's home to such professional teams as the San Diego Padres, the Chargers, and the Gulls. The Del Mar Thoroughbred Club hosts horse racing each summer at the Del Mar Race Track, where the "turf meets the surf." Or you can catch a polo match at the San Diego Polo Club. Olympic hopefuls train at the ARCO Training Center in Chula Vista. San Diego has played host to some of the biggest athletic competitions in the world, from the America's Cup to the Super Bowl, and to some of the best athletes, from native son Phil Mickelson to Tiger Woods. Professional golfers come to San Diego for beautiful courses and big bucks. Major tournaments, such as the Accenture Match Play Championship, are played here.

San Diego is also a resort town, with 70 miles of sand and surf stretching all the way from the Mexican border to the seaside communities of the North County. There are more than two dozen beaches here, each with its own distinct personality: from Mission Beach, where the summer seems endless (and so do the parties), to the La Jolla Cove, a paradise for scuba divers. On the water, you can surf or sail; in the air, hang-glide or take a hot air balloon ride. With its 90 courses, San Diego is a golfer's dream. And where else can you find an average daytime temperature of 70 degrees? No wonder San Diego's reputation is spreading abroad as a world-class tourist destination.

San Diego is home to such attractions as SeaWorld, the World Famous San Diego Zoo, Wild Animal Park, and Legoland. It has 90 museums, including the San Diego Museum of Art, and theatres such as the Old Globe. Adding to the city's rich cultural life are the San Diego Symphony, Opera, Repertory Theatre, the Museum of Contemporary Art, the La Jolla Playhouse, and the California Center for the Arts.

San Diego calls itself "America's Finest City." Think it's just a slick, advertising slogan? Just ask the people who live here–or better yet, those who wish they did.

Downtown

The modern city of San Diego was founded by Alonzo E. Horton, a merchant from San Francisco who arrived here aboard the steamer, *Pacific*, in 1867. In her book on Horton, Elizabeth C. MacPhail writes, "He was asked where he thought the city should be. 'Right down there by the wharf,' Horton said. 'I have been nearly all over the United States and that is the prettiest place for a city I ever saw. Is there any land for sale?'" Luckily for us–there was.

Horton bought up 960 acres at auction for $265–a bargain at about 27 cents an acre–and San Diego's downtown was born. But according to the San Diego Historical Society, Horton had to shell out an additional $4,000 two years later to add a single parcel to complete his "New Town." Somehow he missed it the first time around. And by the time he realized the error, the land had soared in value.

At first, folks were skeptical that Horton's hopes for a city weren't just another "Davis' Folly." William Heath Davis, a merchant and trader, had tried to build a town on the same spot 17 years earlier. But Horton succeeded where Davis had not.

Despite the eventual success of his New Town, Horton died a poor man, most of his property lost through tax sales and foreclosures. But on his 95th birthday he told a newspaper reporter that the city he helped build was still "the most beautiful place in the world." If he were alive today, Horton would probably feel the same way.

Nowhere is the city's growth more evident than downtown where gleaming office towers climb the horizon, their mirrored glass reflecting both sea and sky.

There are many fine hotels here, including the venerable U.S. Grant, built in 1910, and the elegant Westgate. Along the marina, the Marriott's twin glass towers glitter, the Hyatt Regency scrapes the sky, and the San Diego Convention Center looks like a great ship ready to set sail.

From there, it's a short stroll along the marina walk to **Seaport Village** with 14 acres of shopping and entertainment. Minstrels, mimes, clowns, choral groups and bands often entertain visitors for free. There are more than 55 shops, and four major restaurants, including the Harbor House, all with views of San Diego Bay. For a quick snack, you can choose from more than a dozen fast food eateries, serving everything from grilled swordfish to gyros, ice cream and cappuccino. Dine at tables outside, or better yet, carry your picnic to a grassy spot overlooking the water and the Navy ships moored nearby.

Seaport Village is located at 849 West Harbor Drive at Kettner Boulevard.

Leaving Seaport Village, meander along the boardwalk past the fishing boats to the **Fish Market/Top of the Market**

Downtown Marina, Seaport Village and Convention Center

San Diego Trolley and Condominium towers, Harbor Drive

Convention Center

Restaurant on North Harbor Drive. It has a nautical theme and panoramic harbor views. Upstairs is elegant; downstairs, informal. But on either level, the fish is a standout.

Close by on the **Embarcadero** are the Anthony's restaurants, founded by an Italian fishing family that has been in the business more than 50 years. They include **Anthony's Fish Grotto**–a favorite with seniors and families; the **Star of the Sea Room**–formal with fare to match; and the **Fishette**–"fast fish." Share an order of fried clams with the sea gulls out on the restaurant's wooden deck.

Next door is the **San Diego Maritime Museum**, at 1300 N. Harbor Drive. Here you can tour a trio of ships: the ferryboat *Berkeley*; the steam yacht *Medea*; and the famous *Star of India*, the oldest active sailing vessel in the world. With the wind billowing her sails off Point Loma, the *Star* is a sight to behold. This venerable ship was built on the Isle of Man way back in 1863 of iron instead of wood, the material of choice for vessels of the day. She was christened *Euterpe*, for the Greek Goddess of music. After more than six decades at sea, the *Star* was purchased for $9,000 by a group of San Diegans with a vision.

"It was just a bunch of guys who loved old ships, the old square riggers and the Great Age of Sail," says Joseph Ditler, the museum's development director. "They had this marvelous dream–which was so advanced for its time–and that was to bring the ship to San Diego and build a museum around her." Their dream was delayed: first by the Depression and then by World War II, when the *Star* was in danger of being sold for scrap. It wasn't until the 1950s that the tide changed. On a trip to San Diego, Allen Villiers, a sea captain and well-known author, blasted the city for its neglect and shamed it into restoring this historic treasure. When the *Star* finally set sail again in 1976–during the nation's Bicentennial–a half million people lined the waterfront to see her off. Since then, the *Star* has sailed on many special occasions, including at the Festival of Sail in 1999, which brought fourteen tall ships from around the world to San Diego.

If you're feeling seaworthy after the tour, take a boat ride yourself. Catch a ferry to Coronado Island from the Broadway Pier, or take harbor excursions around San Diego Bay.

In the heart of the city is **Horton Plaza**, a $140 million shopping and entertainment complex that helped to revitalize downtown, turning a decaying business district into a center for both commercial and residential development.

The plaza, named after city father Alonzo Horton, is a sort of open-air urban bazaar, with colorful banners, topiary animals, and a turn-of-the-century clock. Here you'll find pushcart vendors and street performers from mimes to magicians.

The plaza's strong colors and shapes are the work of acclaimed architect Jon Jerde, who designed the 1984 Los Angeles Olympic Games and the Universal CityWalk, among many others. His design for the Horton Plaza is twisting and unpredictable–you never know *what* you'll find around the next corner.

This multi-level plaza stretches for nearly seven city blocks with more than 140 shops and restaurants; a 14-screen cinema; and the **Lyceum Stage and Space**, home to the **San Diego Repertory Theater**. On the top level, grab some fast fare at the food court, or take in the city skyline at the **Napa Valley Grille**, serving wine country cuisine. And if you're tired after all that shopping (and eating), the 450-room **Westin Hotel** is just steps away.

Horton Plaza is located between Broadway and G Street and First and Fourth Avenues.

Close by is the **Gaslamp Quarter** where you can take a stroll into San Diego's past. Wyatt Earp once ran three gambling houses here, and sailors came looking for a good time after long months at sea. The Gaslamp was the city's notorious red light district, known as the "Stingaree." Historians say the name probably came from the stingrays in San Diego Bay. But it was said you could be stung just as badly in the brothels and bars of the Stingaree.

Business boomed. In the late 1880s, the Stingaree had about 70 saloons with names like "Old Tub of Blood" and "First and Last Chance Saloon" and 120 bordellos. Among the hundreds of call girls who made a living here was a feisty redhead, Ida Bailey. In 1903, "Madam" Bailey opened her own brothel in a pale yellow house with a white picket fence. Here she and her girls entertained the city's rich and famous, including the mayor and police chief.

In the mid-1970s merchants and property owners started a movement to save and restore the Gaslamp's Victorian architecture. In 1980 the 16-block area was designated a National Historic District.

Today, little of the Gaslamp's bawdy past remains. Most of the peep shows, topless bars and X-rated bookstores have been replaced with trendy bistros and boutiques. There's a vibrant nightlife, with many new restaurants, clubs, and coffee houses.

Croce's Restaurant & Jazz Bar on Fifth Avenue has been a lively landmark in the Gaslamp since the beginning of the quarter's transformation. Owner Ingrid Croce, widow of the late singer-songwriter, Jim Croce, was among the first entrepreneurs to envision the Gaslamp's potential. Her gamble paid off. Croce's has expanded to two bustling restaurants and three nightclubs. The establishment keeps Jim Croce's legacy alive, entertaining visitors from all over the world with live music and fine food. Son A.J., a pianist and singer, has followed in his famous father's footsteps. He performs at Croce's several times a year.

Ole Madrid, a Spanish restaurant with a disco in the basement, is a favorite on Friday nights, with long lines snaking onto the sidewalk. **Dick's Last Resort** is funky and fun. **Johnny Love's** and the **Bitter End** also pack 'em in.

Italian restaurants predominate in the Gaslamp, with **Panevino** on Fifth, among the local favorites. But here you can find something to fit every taste and budget, from Cajun to continental, Persian to Pacific Rim.

For ribs and beer, belly up to the **Kansas City Barbeque**, a restaurant and watering hole at Market Street and Harbor Drive near the Convention Center. Scenes from the film, "Top Gun" were filmed here. (For some reason the place is decorated with brassieres of all sizes.)

Among the hotels in the Gaslamp is the **Horton Grand**, rebuilt brick by brick from two turn-of-the-century hotels. While amenities are up to date, the hotel borrows from its Victorian past. The bellhops even wear knickers. And the restaurant is named after the Gaslamp's famous madam, Ida Bailey. Guest rooms have period décor, antiques, and cozy fireplaces. Wyatt Earp once slept here, as did President Benjamin Harrison. But perhaps the most infamous hotel guest is a ghost. Roger Whittacre was a gambler back in the 1880s. According to the story, he was shot over a gambling

SEAPORT VILLAGE

Horton Plaza

Opposite: Seaport Village

debt, a woman–or both–while hiding inside an armoire. All this happened at another hotel. But for some reason his ghost calls the Horton Grand home. Roger is said to haunt Room 309. Stay there–if you dare!

The Gaslamp Quarter is bounded by Broadway and L Street, Fourth and Sixth Avenues.

Coronado

From downtown, take the ferry, or drive the long blue curve of bridge over to Coronado Island. As you cross you can catch a breathtaking view of the San Diego skyline with a fleet of boats gently rocking in the foreground. Coronado is an old community that seems a throwback to simpler times. There are elegant, late-19th and early-20th century mansions here, along with neat rows of houses from the 1940s and 50s. On Coronado's Main Street, Orange Avenue, you can spread your blanket by the gazebo in **Spreckels Park**, and listen to a summer concert. Some of San Diego's oldest families live here, along with newer Navy families. Many were so captivated with Coronado during tours here that they returned to retire.

Coronado is rich in naval history–it was here that naval aviation was born. And the Naval Air Station North Island, on the tip of the peninsula, remains one of the most important air and sea complexes on the West Coast. During World War II, it was a vital training, staging, and development center for ships and air squadrons.

Charles Lindbergh flew the *Spirit of St. Louis* from North Island on May 10, 1927, on the first leg of his history-making transatlantic flight. The plane was financed by businessmen from St. Louis but built in San Diego.

But Coronado is best known for the **Hotel del Coronado**– "The Del" to locals. This grand old Victorian, with its red-roofed turrets, has been a local landmark for more than a century and recently underwent a $50 million restoration. Ten presidents have slept here; the movie, *Some Like It Hot* was filmed here; and generations of tourists have flocked to the Del's broad sweep of beach.

The Hotel Del was built at a time when President Grover Cleveland ran the White House, and Wyatt Earp ran Tombstone. Railroad tycoon Elisha Babcock and his partner, piano magnate H.L. Story, wanted to build a resort hotel that would be the "talk of the Western World."

The Del opened on February 19, 1888. At a cost of more than a million dollars, it was the most expensive hotel on the West Coast–and the largest structure, outside of New York City with electric lights. This was such newfangled stuff that each guest room had a card that advised: "This room is equipped with the Edison Electric Light. Do not attempt to light with a match. Simply turn key on the wall by the door. The use of electricity for lighting is in no way harmful to health, nor does it affect soundness of sleep."

Over the years, this National Historic Landmark has been visited by the famous and infamous and–legend has it–by the ghost of Kate Morgan. She was a beautiful young woman who checked into the hotel in 1892, but never checked out. Her body was found on a stairway leading to the beach, with a pistol close by. Was it murder or suicide? The debate continues to this day. Some claim Kate's ghost "haunts" Room 3327.

Over the years witnesses have reported unexplained sights and sounds: flickering lights, strange footsteps, a television set that turns itself on and off, curtains that billow in the breeze even when the windows are closed. Paranormal

The Horton Grand Hotel

The Gaslamp Quarter

researchers have used infrared cameras, night vision glasses, sensors and sound detectors to document the ghostly goings-on. They have recorded temperature fluctuations, magnetic fields, electronic emissions, and other "paranormal" activity, but all of them remain a mystery.

The Del has also been host to presidents and princes, magnates and movie stars, heroes and heads of state. It was the site of a formal dinner honoring Charles Lindbergh after his historic transatlantic flight. And it was here that the Prince of Wales is rumored to have met Wallis Simpson during a glittering gala in 1920. She was then the wife of the commanding officer of nearby Naval Station North Island. Sixteen years later, King Edward VII gave up his throne to marry "the woman I love."

Inspired by their love story, the **Prince of Wales** restaurant (one of eight restaurants and lounges at the Del) offers romantic dining, both indoors and out. This elegant spot is as glamorous as the Windsors themselves, with walls striped in taupe, gold and cream, luxurious banquettes, and a long limestone bar. Have a drink (or just drink in the view) as the sun sinks into the Pacific. Then enjoy classic cuisine by candlelight.

You don't have to be a royal to dine in the Del's **Crown Room**, but you'll feel like one. This majestic room has a curved pine ceiling that soars 30 feet high. You feel as though you've been swallowed up by some immense whale. Something of an engineering marvel, it has no nails or interior supports: it's held together entirely with wooded pegs. Topping it all off are four chandeliers shaped like crowns. The Crown Room is open for Sunday brunch, holidays, and special events.

The Del's **Sheerwater Restaurant** has three levels of outdoor terrace seating to give you unparalleled white water views. Fireplaces outside keep you toasty even when there's a chill in the air. Select from California coastal cuisine, along with pizza baked in a giant wood-burning oven.

The adjoining bar, called **Babcock and Story**, after the Del's founders, features cocktails and oysters, both indoors and out.

In the lobby's **Palm Court**, you can sink into a Victorian-style chair and order light fare, cocktails, or coffee and pastries. On Sunday afternoons, there's a traditional High Tea. At Christmas time, the wood-paneled lobby lights up with a magnificent tree soaring several stories high.

The "**Windsor Lawn**," a grand carpet of green, beckons guests with landscaped walkways and seaside sitting areas. Its centerpiece is Windsor Cottage, where Wallace Simpson once lived. This California beach bungalow, built in 1905, was relocated to the Del, where it is now used for special events, parties, and weddings.

For recreation, the Del has two pools, tennis courts, an oceanfront Spa and Fitness Center with state-of-the-art equipment and the latest in spa treatments and services. There's also a salon and shopping gallery. And across the street at the Del's Marina, you can rent a sailboat, jet-ski, or kayak.

Over the generations, the white and red gazebo in the garden patio has been the setting for countless weddings. It is one of many special places that lend the Del a sense of history.

So pull up a wicker chair, or stroll the paths along the beach. And drink in the sweet scent of jasmine and geraniums. This is the place to loll your days away, at this grand lady by the sea.

Head south out of the Del onto Silver Strand Boulevard (it becomes Highway 75), and you'll soon come to the **Loews**

Coronado Bay Resort. It's on a private peninsula surrounded by water and has its own 80-slip marina where you can rent sailboats and wave runners or catch a water taxi to Coronado and San Diego Harbor. The resort's **Market Café**, overlooking the colorful marina, offers dining inside and al fresco. The restaurant has an airy feeling, filled with wood and wicker. At the adjoining **Market Deli**, they'll pack a gourmet picnic for beach or boat.

The more formal **Azzura Point Restaurant** upstairs is both elegant and exotic with its Venetian-style chandeliers, suede-and-silk draperies and animal-print accents. Bay front windows offer sweeping views of the Coronado Bay Bridge and the San Diego skyline. Dine on California-Mediterranean cuisine as you watch the city lights shimmer across the bay. At the adjoining **Azzura Point Bar**, you can savor Spanish *tapas* along with a San Diego sunset.

Besides its "Sea Spa," the resort has a 10,000 square foot spa, a salon and fitness center, tennis courts, a putting green, three swimming pools and whirlpools. Take surfing lessons from "Kahuna Bob," charter a yacht or take a romantic gondola ride on the canals nearby. You can learn how to dance the salsa, take in a "dive in" movie, or roast marshmallows on the beach. And the resort's chefs even lead guests on late night "refrigerator raids."

On the other side of the peninsula, the **Coronado Island Marriott Resort** covers 16 acres along the waterfront near the foot of the Coronado Bay Bridge. Here you'll find breathtaking views of both bay and skyline. The resort has 300 rooms and suites, and villas with their own pool.

L'Escale restaurant has a Mediterranean feel, with heavy wood side tables and tile floors. You can dine in or outside, overlooking the pool and the bustling bay beyond, where sailboats mingle with merchant ships. Or do some mingling yourself at the clubby La Provence, a stylish spot for an aperitif.

The Marriott has six tennis courts, three pools and a hot tub, a weight room, and a spa to spoil you. There's also jet skiing, sailing, and deep-sea fishing. You can bike or stroll along the broad paths overlooking the bay, or hail a water taxi to restaurants and shopping in San Diego.

Not far away is the **Ferry Landing Marketplace** with dozens of shops and cafes, **Il Fornaio** and **Peohe's Restaurant**, known for its spectacular view.

The ferry departs from San Diego's Broadway Pier every hour from 7:00 a.m. to 10:00 p.m. (11:00 p.m. on Fridays and Saturdays) every day of the year.

Hotel Del Coronado

San Diego skyline from Coronado

Coronado Bridge

Old Point Loma Lighthouse

Balboa Park

Balboa Park, one of the largest urban parks in the country, has lush grounds and botanical gardens stretching over 1,400 acres. It's a delightful place to spread your blanket and while away a summer's day, explore the many museums, or meander along the walkways. There's a bit of magic at every turn: actors performing Shakespeare in a garden grotto; children splashing in a fountain; Spanish music drifting through the trees. The park's hundred-bell carillon tolls hour after hour. Even so, there's a sense of timelessness here.

The beautiful old Spanish-Moorish buildings were constructed for the Panama-California International Exposition of 1915-1916, to celebrate the opening of the Panama Canal. They were intended as temporary structures, but the city fathers made the buildings a permanent part of the park, and later construction followed the original Spanish theme.

Stroll **El Prado**, the park's "main street," lined with museums. Here you'll find native dancers and musicians, palm readers and painters. (*December Nights* on the Prado has become a San Diego tradition. Museum admissions are free, and there's festive food and entertainment.)

Just past the lily pond, sometimes teaming with tadpoles, is the **Botanical Building**, a grand wooden "birdcage" filled with exotic plants. Continue down El Prado to the plaza where you'll find the **San Diego Museum of Art**, and the **House of Hospitality** with an information office.

Hang a left and head for the **Spreckels Organ** and Pavilion. At the opening of the Panama-California Exposition, sugar magnates John D. and Adolph Spreckels gave the city this colossal gift. The Spreckels pipe organ is considered to be the world's largest outdoor musical instrument. At times, this concert organ can be heard two miles away. It takes a 20-horsepower electric blower to provide the huge volume of air the organ requires. And what a set of pipes–about 4,500 to be exact. There are free public concerts every Sunday afternoon at 2 p.m., as well as evening concerts during the summer.

If you make a right at the Organ Pavilion, you'll see the **Hall of Nations** and the **House of Pacific Relations**, a cluster of cottages devoted to the cultures of different nations: China, Czechoslovakia, Germany, Hungary, Ireland, Israel, Norway, and others. The cottages are open on weekends, and, on national holidays, celebrations are often held in the center courtyard.

Among the many museums in the park: the **Reuben H. Fleet Space Theatre and Science Center** shows large-format Omnimax films; the **San Diego Museum of Art** has a permanent collection that includes Indian and Asian art, masterpieces by El Greco, Goya, Matisse, O'Keefe, and Toulouse-Lautrec as well as cutting-edge California artists; the **San Diego Natural History Museum** features exhibits on dinosaurs, minerals, the ocean, seashore, and desert, not to mention California's endangered species; and the **San Diego Aerospace Museum** and **International Aerospace Hall** of Fame traces flight from its birth through the space age with exhibits on aviation heroes. It even has a moon rock.

If all that museum hopping makes you hungry, grab a light lunch at the **Sculpture Garden Cafe** by the San Diego Museum of Art or at **The Prado**, a restaurant open for both lunch and dinner in the House of Hospitality.

For entertainment, the **Simon Edison Centre for the Performing Arts** includes the **Lowell Davies Festival Theatre**, the **Cassius Carter Centre Stage**, and the **Old Globe Theatre**, which offers both classic and contemporary works, as well as the summer Shakespeare Festival. The **Starlight Bowl** presents summer musicals in its outdoor amphitheater. And the **Casa del Prado Theatre** hosts the Junior Theatre, Youth Symphony, and the San Diego Gilbert and Sullivan Company.

San Diego Zoo

"The World Famous San Diego Zoo" (that's the official name) started out with a handful of specimens inherited from the 1915-1916 Panama-California International Exposition. The Zoo has grown to one of the world's biggest and best–a 100-acre tropical garden with 4,000 animals representing 800 species. Most live in enclosures that look, and even sound, like their natural homes in the wild.

The *Gorilla Tropics*, for instance, has the best stereo system in town. Lowland gorillas hear the primitive sounds of a rain forest recorded on location in Africa. Compact discs play the sounds on dozens of speakers hidden throughout the enclosure. The exhibit covers 2.5 acres filled with waterfalls, pools, and plants. There's even a cavernous free flight aviary, with hundreds of exotic African birds. You'll go ape over it all.

The *Ituri Forest* is a four-acre tropical jungle filled with hippos, forest buffalos, colorful birds and monkeys. The most complex habitat at the zoo, it takes visitors along winding trails through thick rain forests and bamboo passageways. A 150,000-gallon pool resembles an African marsh–home to a pair of hippos. Believe it or not these two-ton animals can swim, and gracefully.

The *Polar Bear Plunge* is home to the great white bears of the arctic and some of their "friends"–Siberian reindeer, arctic foxes, and northern birds. This habitat, which brings the tundra to tropical San Diego, features a giant pool where, to the delight of visitors, the ice bears swim. You can watch it all from underwater viewing areas that offer fisheye views of this fascinating arctic world.

Tiger River takes you on a trip through a three-acre Asian rain forest. You'll see hundreds of mammals, reptiles, and birds, including Chinese water dragons, Malayan tapirs, and Sumatran tigers. Besides the fauna, there's a half million dollars worth of exotic flowers and plants. Here, Mother Nature gets a little help from high technology–a computer-controlled fogging system creates mist and humidity not normally found in San Diego's dry climate.

The *Sun Bear Forest* is like a big playpen for these mischievous Malayan bears, tree dwellers from Southeast Asia and Borneo. The bears "trashed" their multi-million dollar enclosure. So the zoo had to remodel it. It's now "bear-proof." These comical bears, masters of clowning around, are real crowd pleasers.

And don't forget the koalas, which are among the most popular critters in the zoo. Their colony here is the largest outside Australia. In fact, these cuddly creatures have become synonymous with the San Diego Zoo, the first in this country to exhibit them.

Kids of all ages will love the *Children's Zoo* with its "petting paddock," walk-through bird aviaries, and nurseries where baby animals rejected by their mothers are bottle fed and cared for by their keepers.

All of San Diego fell in love with one of the Zoo's newer additions, Hua Mei, a giant panda cub born there in August 1999. It was a momentous occasion–the first of this

A koala at the San Diego Zoo

The zoo is cool!

The Immaculata, University of San Diego

Cabrillo National Monument

endangered species to be born in the Western Hemisphere in 10 years. The whole world got a good look at the infant via the Internet. There was so much interest, that the Zoo launched the live "Panda Cam" on its website. The panda has since been sent to the People's Republic of China where the Zoo's Center for Reproduction of Endangered Species (CRES) is working to save these beloved creatures and their mountain habitat. Hua Mei's Mom and Dad, Bai Yun and Shi Shi, were on a long-term research loan from the People's Republic of China. CRES scientists are collaborating with Chinese scientists to learn how giant pandas behave and reproduce.

You can see the Zoo by bus on guided tours, or by air, 180 feet up. The Skyfari aerial tram will take you for a gondola ride over the treetops. Hungry? There's plenty of feeding time for both animals and humans (from hot dogs and sodas to finer fare.)

The Zoo is operated by the nonprofit Zoological Society of San Diego, which also manages the San Diego Wild Animal Park. The Zoo is open daily from 9 a.m. to 4 p.m. with extended summer hours.

The San Diego Zoo is located in Balboa Park at Park Boulevard and Zoo Place.

Old Town

Old Town is San Diego's birthplace. It was little more than a collection of ramshackle buildings and adobe houses when the city was incorporated in 1850. But the area's colorful history begins long before that.

The first San Diegans were Indians who called themselves the Tipai and Ipai, names that translate as "people," according to the anthropologists. The Spaniards called them "San Dieguenos" and set about Christianizing them.

On July 16, 1769, Father Junipero Serra founded the first California Mission, called **San Diego de Alcala**, on Presidio Hill overlooking what is now Old Town. That site did not have adequate water, however, so the mission was moved to its present location on the San Diego River. A fire and two earthquakes destroyed most of the original structures, but Father Serra's living quarters and the church facade survived. You can visit the rebuilt mission, and the museum, chapel, and gardens at 10818 San Diego Mission Road in Mission Valley.

For 50 years, life in San Diego centered on the mission and presidio, or fort. But gradually soldiers and other settlers moved down the hill to Old Town where there were plots of land to cultivate. In the early 1820s, a plaza was laid out as the center of this new settlement. Over the next 15 years, the town grew steadily. In the mid-1830s, Richard Henry Dana Jr. described Old Town as "about 40 dark brown looking huts ... and three or four larger ones, white-washed, which belonged to the 'gente de razon,'" which is to say, the upper class. As the settlement grew, the Presidio declined and was eventually abandoned.

Over the years, San Diego changed hands several times: first in 1821, when Mexico won independence from Spain and again in 1848, when the Treaty of Guadalupe-Hidalgo put California, Texas, and New Mexico under U.S. control.

Old Town grew for a time under the Americans. But gradually Alonzo Horton's New Town near the wharf attracted commerce and became the center of San Diego. To make matters worse for Old Town, a fire in 1872 destroyed many of its buildings. Today six square blocks of historic buildings, shops, and restaurants offer glimpses of its past.

The **Whaley House** on San Diego Avenue, built in 1856, is Southern California's first two-story brick building. Though modest by today's standards, it was considered a mansion back then. Businessman Thomas Whaley, whose spirit is said to make appearances now and then, built it. June Reading, the late director of the Whaley House, used to give visitors an earful.

"This house is alive," she once told me, "with noises and sounds and fragrances." Reading claimed she, herself, had seen Whaley. She described him as "a short man in a black frock coat, black pantaloons, and a broad-brimmed hat." And at times, the odor of his favorite Havana cigars is said to waft through the main hall.

Others say they've seen Whaley's wife, Anna. Witnesses swear they've smelled her heavy, sweet perfume or heard the rustle of her skirts on the stairs. Even the family's pet terrier, Dolly Varden, has been seen running through the house, only to disappear. Or at least, that's what they say.

If that's not enough spirits for one house, Yankee Jim Robinson is reported to walk the floor upstairs. He was hanged in 1852 on the spot where Whaley later built his house. It was a stiff sentence for trying to steal a schooner worth $6,500. Yankee Jim thought the authorities were just trying to scare him, but he was dead wrong. And he must have died with his boots on. June Reading claimed that footsteps on the second floor sounded like "a big man wearing boots."

Whether you believe any of the stories or not, the Whaley House is listed on the U.S. Department of Commerce catalog of 30 ghost houses in the United States, one of only two in California.

Besides its original role as the Whaley family home, the house has served as a granary, country store, church, courthouse, public school, and the first theatre in town. Today you can tour the courtroom and parlor on the first floor and the antique-furnished bedrooms on the second. Maybe you'll even see Thomas Whaley if you're lucky.

Down the street from The Whaley House is the **Old Town State Historic Park**, a collection of restored and reconstructed buildings that recreate California life from 1821 to 1872. Walking tours begin every day at 11 a.m. and 2 p.m. You can explore adobe houses, haciendas, a blacksmith's shop, and a restored newspaper office where the first edition of the *San Diego Union* came off the press in 1868.

Another point of historical interest is **La Casa de Estudillo**, an adobe house considered one of the finest remnants of Mexican California. A retired presidio *commandante* began construction in 1827 but died before it was completed. His son continued the work. Rooms are laid out around a central courtyard, including a *sala,* or family room, a study, bedrooms, and a chapel. Food was prepared outside in the kitchen area under a veranda. Rooms have beamed ceilings, whitewashed walls, and brick floors. Furnishings include original pieces from the Mexican and Early American periods, as well as reproductions.

The **Mason Street School House**, built in 1865, was San Diego's first. Mary Chase Walker, the first teacher, had a salary of $65 a month. But she retired after less than a year to marry the head of the school board. More than a 100 years later, this one-room schoolhouse is still used for education: adult classes in California history are taught there.

Seeley Stable includes a reconstructed stable and barns housing a collection of horse-drawn vehicles, western

Junipero Serra Museum

Opposite: Mission San Diego de Acala

memorabilia, and Indian artifacts, some of them thousands of years old. In 1867, Albert Seeley started the San Diego-Los Angeles Stage Line. His stagecoaches made the 130-mile journey in less than 24 hours, a trip that now takes about three.

La Casa de Bandini, a beautiful hacienda built in 1829 for Juan Bandini, was a social center during Mexican rule. It was later sold to Albert Seeley, who added a second floor and opened the Cosmopolitan Hotel. Now it houses a popular restaurant. Citrus trees, birds of paradise, and palms frame the central courtyard. You can sit outside under green-striped umbrellas, and listen to strolling mariachis while you sip a margarita.

And don't miss **Bazaar del Mundo**, a colorful collection of shops and restaurants laid out around a courtyard, abloom with plants and flowers. On weekends Spanish and Mexican dancers add to the festive atmosphere. And many of the shops sell Mexican folk arts and crafts. There are several restaurants to choose from, including **Casa de Pico**, known for good, inexpensive food and "grande" margaritas.

The bazaar is located near the plaza at Juan and Wallace streets.

Other Old Town restaurants are **Cafe Pacifica**, consistently rated one of the finest for fish, and the Old Town Mexican Cafe, where you can watch tortillas being made while you wait for a table. Both are on San Diego Avenue.

Next door to the cafe is the **Old Town Esplanade**, a two-level shopping complex where stores sell everything from stuffed bears to Birkenstock sandals. There's also **Café Coyote**, a restaurant and bar.

Climb up Harney Street to **Heritage Park** and its collection of restored Victorian houses and other buildings. They now house offices, shops, and the **Heritage Park Inn**, a bed and breakfast.

To complete your tour, take a winding road up to **Presidio Park**, overlooking Old Town. The original buildings no longer exist, but tiles from the Presidio chapel were salvaged and used to fashion a 28-foot cross on the site. At the **Junipero Serra Museum and Library**, exhibits trace the adventures of Indians, Spanish explorers and priests, and the first Mexican and American settlers. This 40-acre park is also a favorite with picnickers–and lovers–who sit on its grassy slopes and watch the city bustle below them–a city that was born in Old Town.

From I-5, take the Old Town Avenue exit, and turn left on San Diego Avenue. Or take the trolley.

SeaWorld

SeaWorld, a 189-acre adventure park, is one of the most visited of all San Diego attractions, offering shows, exhibits, aquariums and rides. Shamu, its most famous finny creature, performs to delighted crowds in Shamu Stadium. Sit in the first 14 rows, and you're sure to get wet! Shamu Vision, a 30-square-foot TV screen, gives you a good view no matter where you sit.

There are also dolphins, sea lions, otters, walruses, exotic marine birds, sea turtles–and sharks! The Shark Encounter has the world's largest display of sharks–more than 400 of them glide through nearly 280,000 gallons of saltwater.

Pirates 4-D features a film about a wacky captain and his hapless band of swashbucklers. The audience wears 3-D glasses and watches the action on a giant screen. You're drawn into the adventure by special effects that SeaWorld describes as "in-your-face" entertainment.

Shipwreck Rapids, SeaWorld's first adventure ride, is making waves with crowds. Imagine yourself a castaway trying to return to civilization. Nine-passenger rafts take you spinning along a winding river, plunging through a forbidding tunnel, and dodging obstacles that will give you thrills (if not spills). At the end of your voyage, you can grab a bite at the Shipwreck Reef Cave amid lush tropical gardens, as sea lions and other animals entertain you.

Wild Arctic takes you on an exciting, simulated helicopter ride to the top of the world, a base station in the Arctic, inhabited by polar bears, beluga whales, arctic foxes, seals and other animals. Crowds go wild when the great white bears go paddling in their swimming pool and the immense walruses glide about in a surprisingly graceful water ballet. Spectators can watch both above and below water, often coming nose-to-nose when these marine mammals swim close to the windows.

Other attractions include *Rocky Point Preserve*, where visitors can interact with bottlenose dolphin; the *Penguin Encounter*, with more than 350 Antarctic penguins in a frosty, 25-degree environment; *Forbidden Reef*, where you can feed bat rays in a shallow lagoon and come face to face with eerie moray eels; and–always a favorite–the sea lion and otter show starring Clyde and Seamore.

Feed the fish or feed your face at the many fast food restaurants and snack bars.

You can take a six-minute sky ride over Mission Bay or see all of SeaWorld and San Diego on the *Skytower*, a 320-foot spiral into the sky. If you want to keep your feet on the ground, go for a guided walking tour.

SeaWorld is located off I-5 on SeaWorld Drive. Park hours vary by season.

Mission Bay & Mission Beach

Not far away is **Mission Bay Park**, a favorite recreation spot for families. Here the waters are shallow and sheltered for swimming. Sailing and windsurfing are also popular. There are grassy places for family picnics, playgrounds for kids, and miles of sidewalks for strolling. On breezy afternoons, kite-flyers will dazzle you with their aerobatics. Mission Bay Park is off Mission Boulevard, West Mission Bay Drive, and Ingraham Street.

Perhaps San Diego's most visited strand is **Mission Beach**, a sort of human carnival on the sand. The boardwalk has been compared to a Fellini movie filled with colorful, sometimes bizarre people. There's South Mission Beach where San Diego State students major in volleyball. And there's North Mission where, says local television personality Larry Himmel, "you're never too old to surf or too young to skateboard." I agree with Larry that Mission Beach "is more than just a place, it's an attitude."

There's also **Belmont Park**, a beach-front amusement center, where you can ride the Giant Dipper, a vintage roller coaster that reaches speeds of 40 to 45 miles per hour. The coaster was built in 1925 for sugar magnate John D. Spreckels at a cost of $150,000. But over the years, it has had its own share of ups and downs. It was closed in 1976, but a coalition of coaster and history buffs won a state historic preservation grant and fought to save it from demolition. The coaster has since been restored to its original condition–but this time the tab was more than $2 million.

Belmont Park has tamer rides including the *Liberty Carousel*; *Pirate's Cove*, an indoor recreation area for kids; and

Santa Fe Passenger Depot

a video game arcade. Or dive into **The Plunge**, the largest indoor pool in southern California.

From I-5 take Highway 8 or SeaWorld Drive west and follow the signs to West Mission Bay Drive.

Point Loma

It's a long trek to the tip of Point Loma and the **Cabrillo National Monument**. But the vista–a spectacular 360-degree view of San Diego Harbor, the ocean, and the mountains–is well worth the drive. It's a perfect place to watch Navy ships sailing into the harbor or planes taking off from Naval Air Station North Island. You might even see gray whales on their annual migration if you visit between late December and late February. Every year, they pass Point Loma on the way from the Arctic Ocean to Baja California, a journey of 5,000 miles. The park also offers exhibits, tours, and films.

The site commemorates Juan Rodriquez Cabrillo, the Portuguese explorer who discovered what is now California on September 28, 1542. Fifty years after Columbus first arrived in the New World, Cabrillo set out on his voyage of discovery from the Mexican port of Navidad. He had a commission to find a sea route to the Atlantic Ocean, around what was then believed to be the island of California. His patron, the Viceroy of Mexico, Antonio de Mendoza, was motivated by the glitter of gold and the legend of Queen Califia. According to myth, she ruled an island kingdom inhabited by Amazon warriors who carried swords of gold because they had no other metal.

Cabrillo found no gold, but what he did find was ultimately far more valuable: the 800 miles of coastline that stretch from Baja to Oregon–not to mention Santa Catalina, San Clemente, and San Miguel islands. But Cabrillo's quest brought on his demise. He broke his leg and died from complications six weeks later. His statue now looks out over the ocean he sailed, the coastline he discovered.

While you're here, be sure to tour the **Old Point Loma Lighthouse** built in 1855. Although it guided ships into San Diego Harbor for 36 years, it was deemed ineffective because of the thick clouds and fog that often shrouded it. In 1891, it was retired and replaced by a newer, less picturesque, but more effective lighthouse nearer the water.

La Jolla

La Jolla means "the jewel" in Spanish, and for residents and visitors alike, this seaside town is a gem. A century ago it attracted a colony of artists who tried to capture its rocky shores and special light. Today it's a wealthy community, where property values have made it a posh playground for townspeople and tourists alike. Even though La Jolla has a cosmopolitan feel, the city fathers (and mothers) have tried hard to retain its village character and charm.

Stroll along palm-lined Prospect, browse in the boutiques and art galleries, or dine al fresco at the many restaurants here. **George's at the Cove**, with three tiers of dining, and **Top of the Cove** are favorites not only for the food, but the view. The locals gather at **Pannikin** for steaming cups of coffee, scones, and croissants. And at the **Hard Rock Cafe**, filled with rock music memorabilia, the waitresses are straight out of central casting: they serve up a lot of ham with the burgers. Directly across the street, **Roppongi Restaurant** serves eclectic Asian cuisine and seafood specialties in a stylish setting. Try the Asian *tapas*, or appetizers, such as the

The cove at La Jolla

Opposite: Beautiful aerial view of La Jolla

Polynesian Dungeness crab stack, which is meant to be shared as well as savored.

Owner Sami Ladeki also founded the Sammy's California Wood-fired Pizza restaurants, and **HotelParisi,** a small, luxury hotel just up the street. For a bit of culture, there's the **Museum of Contemporary Art**, San Diego, with its permanent collection of post-1950 art.

The town's centerpiece is the wonderful old Spanish-style **La Valencia Hotel**, with its pink stucco and bougainvillea. As you enter, you'll pass beneath the colonnade with a palm-shaded **Tropical Patio** to your left and the adjoining **Mediterranean Room** restaurant. The lobby is Spanish tile, with a huge bouquet of flowers on the marble-topped table. Off the lobby, **La Sala**, an elegant drawing room with a floor-to-ceiling window, overlooks La Jolla Cove. Sink into a comfortable chair and drink in the view–or have a drink outside on the Ocean View Terrace. Meals are served as well, weather permitting.

La Valencia's **Whaling Bar & Grill** is a popular watering hole. This dark, cozy tavern has a collection of New Bedford harpoons, scrimshaw, model ships, and murals by Wing Howard. **The Sky Room Restaurant** on the 10th floor offers a lofty look at the La Jolla shoreline. This plush little place has only a dozen tables, a prix fixe menu, and a dazzling 180-degree view of the Pacific.

La Valencia opened on December 15, 1926, soon attracting the wealthy and celebrated. In those days, a room cost as much as $10 a day. Sounds like a bargain now, but back then, it was a week's pay. During the 1930s, La Valencia was a hideaway for Hollywood stars: Charlie Chaplin, Greta Garbo, Lillian Gish, Groucho Marx, Mary Pickford, the Talmadge sisters.

When the **La Jolla Playhouse** was founded in 1947, La Valencia became the gathering place for a new generation of stars: playhouse founders Gregory Peck, Dorothy McGuire, and Mel Ferrer along with Ginger Rogers, Jennifer Jones, and David Niven. Peck was artistic director for a time. And on opening nights, he hosted cast parties in the Whaling Bar.

Over the years, the Valencia has had a loyal following. It's a gathering place for San Diegans as well as visitors. Many weddings and other special occasions, marking time and tradition, have been celebrated here.

When you're finished exploring La Valencia, take a stroll around **La Jolla Cove**, with its lovely palm-lined park overlooking the surf, a sanctuary for fish and wildlife. You can watch the sea lions sun themselves on the rocks, or sun yourself on the beach. Swim and snorkel in the underwater preserve, one of the prime places in San Diego to see marine life. Farther south is **Windansea Beach**, which figured prominently in *The Pumphouse Gang*, Tom Wolfe's take on teen surf culture in the 1960s.

The highest point in La Jolla is **Mount Soledad**, site of a cross that's become a local landmark. From here you have a breathtaking view of the coast.

Take Torrey Pines Road out of town, and stop in the beach and bedroom community of **La Jolla Shores**. There's a short main street with surf shops and other stores, and **Piatti's**, a chic little restaurant. On hot summer days it seems as if all of La Jolla flocks here to bake on the sand, stroll the strand, or picnic in the park. Don't miss the **Marine Room** for dinner or a drink. Its ocean view is one of the best in town: a wall of windows frames the waves. One day back in the 80s the day's catch must have been especially fresh. When high winds and heavy surf smashed through the glass, the restaurant became, temporarily, an aquarium.

Next door is the private **La Jolla Beach and Tennis Club** where the waiting list to join is five years long. But rooms and suites are available to the public. The club has a dozen tennis courts, a pool, a nine-hole executive golf course, and fitness center. The club's dining room is open year-round, but only to members and hotel guests. If you're one of them, a waiter will serve you right on the sand during the summer. The hotel staff will even set up your beach chair and umbrella. Or you can have your own barbeque on the beach.

The **Sea Lodge** next door has a pool, sauna and fitness center and **The Shores** restaurant. Not on the beach, but with breathtaking views is the **Hotel La Jolla at the Shores**. The hotel's **Crescent Shores Grill** on the 11th floor offers a sweeping vista of the La Jolla shoreline along with California cuisine.

Back on North Torrey Pines Road, stop in at the prestigious **Stephen Birch Aquarium-Museum** a little farther north along the coast. This $14-million facility has a panoramic view of the Pacific, man-made tide pools, and an interactive museum. It's part of the world famous Scripps Institution of Oceanography at the University of California, San Diego.

The aquarium is to the right of the galleria, just past a tank filled with silvery sardines. There are more than 60 tanks in all (the biggest, 70,000 gallons) filled with technicolor fish. Taking a tour through the aquarium is a little like taking a voyage with Scripps scientists. Here, you can explore the waters of the Pacific Northwest, Southern California, Mexico's Sea of Cortez, and the South Pacific. In one display, moon jellyfish look like translucent parachutes drifting through space. In another, pink and silver fish dance an aquatic ballet. You'll see brilliant orange garibaldi, gigantic grouper, the flowery tentacles of the sand rose anemone, and rainbow-colored fish cavorting in a coral reef.

The centerpiece of the facility is the giant kelp forest, a 70,000-gallon tank (16 feet deep), filled with marine life from off the coast of La Jolla. Designers used underwater photographs to come up with an exhibit that looks like the real thing. You can view it all through a 13-foot acrylic wall, weighing in at 10 tons.

To the left of the galleria is the museum, with a permanent exhibition on oceanography, *Exploring the Blue Planet*. Here you can learn about earthquakes, weather patterns, and ocean life. The museum has all manner of scientific exhibits, many of them hands-on, including a wave machine (where you can make your own) and the *Ocean Supermarket*, a sort of shoppers' guide to products from the sea. Using a scanner gun, you can "read" the bar codes on products you'd find in your local grocery. You learn that frosting and fudge sauce, for instance, contain seaweed. The display shows how our lives are closely linked to the sea.

The Stephen Birch Aquarium is located at 2300 Expedition Way.

Wind your way along North Torrey Pines Road, past the **Salk Institute** and the **Torrey Pines Glider Port** where hang-gliders take to the skies, soaring off sandstone cliffs overlooking the ocean. Continue on, and you'll pass the **Scripps Clinic and Research Foundation,** along with the **Hilton La Jolla Torrey Pines Hotel** (don't miss the Friday night seafood buffet at the hotel's **Torreyana Grille**), the

Torrey Pines State Reserve

Parasailing at Torrey Pines

Torrey Pines Golf Course, and **Torrey Pines State Reserve**.

All take their name from the twisted *pinus torreyana*, the rarest pine tree in the United States. It now grows only on this reserve and on Santa Rosa Island off the coast near Santa Barbara. The reserve also has a museum with exhibits of its natural and cultural history. In addition, a half-dozen hiking trails snake for seven miles through the pines, offering spectacular views of the Pacific and other natural features–baroque sandstone formations, spring flowers and the famous Torrey Pines themselves.

Some of the trails lead to the very edge of the sandstone cliffs overlooking the ocean below. Another route takes you down to the beach on a narrow, precipitous trail. Take a stroll on the sand and look up at the cliffs, worn by wind and water, and striped with terra cotta, ochre, and verdigris. You can sun yourself on Flat Rock, or poke through the tide pools. Another quarter mile south is Black's Beach where swimsuits are definitely optional. Nudity is banned here, but that doesn't prevent sunbathers from baring and braving it all anyway. (Bring some extra sunscreen.)

To reach the trails and museum, you can drive up the hill or park your car at the base and hoof it. The rules are strict: no smoking, campfires, picnics or pets permitted. And forget the souvenirs. Leave plants, animals, and rocks behind for fellow travelers to enjoy.

Del Mar

From Torrey Pines State Reserve it's a five-minute drive to the charming beach community of Del Mar, "of the sea" in Spanish. This is a small town with expensive homes and expansive views. The town's main street, Camino Del Mar, is lined with boutiques, surf shops, restaurants, and–that's right, you guessed it–real estate offices.

At the north end of of town is **Del Mar Plaza**, a chic shopping and dining complex just blocks from the ocean. There you can settle into an Adirondack chair on the plaza overlooking the Pacific. It's beautifully accented with terra cotta pots abloom with flowers, artwork, and fountains where sculptured "people" take a dip on a hot summer's day. (They look so authentic you'll do a double take.)

Sip vino or cappuccino at **Enoteca** ("wine library" in Italian) or belly up to its take-out bar and order antipasto or *panini*. You can also dine in (or out) at the many good restaurants and bars here. All are prime spots for ocean or people watching: **Il Fornaio** for Italian, **Epazote** for Southwestern, **Pacifica Del Mar** for inventive seafood with the taste of the Pacific Rim. The **Pacifica Breeze Café** is a hang-out for locals who line up for the salmon hash for weekend brunch or the blackened salmon sandwich for lunch. Or you can pick up a picnic at the market, with its selection of sandwiches, soups, salads and pates. The Plaza also has upscale men's and women's boutiques, jewelry and gift shops.

Across the street is **L'Auberge Del Mar Resort and Spa**, a small, elegant hotel overlooking, and within easy walking distance, of the beach. It's on the site of the original Stratford Inn, which later became the Hotel Del Mar, a haven for Hollywood stars. Douglas Fairbanks Sr. and Mary Pickford were frequent guests, as were Charlie Chaplin, tennis great Bill Tilden, Jack Dempsey, George Burns and Gracie Allen.

The present hotel borrows from the past. Off the lobby, the Jimmy Durante Pub is dedicated to the unofficial mayor of Del Mar "in memory of many happy evenings around the piano at the original Hotel Del Mar." Durante used to have a beach house and was a frequent visitor to the nearby Del Mar Race Track. Today, in the pub that bears his name, you can peruse old pictures of him and other Hollywood stars. The pub has a massive, double-sided brick fireplace, a replica of one found in the old hotel. The library and music room is dedicated to Desi Arnaz, who shared a nearby beach home with Lucille Ball. **The Dining Room at L'Auberge** serves California Wine Country cuisine.

In the hotel lobby, settle into a comfortable couch or overstuffed chair and listen to music from the baby grand. French doors lead to a terrace overlooking a landscaped garden and pool with the blue Pacific beyond. L'Auberge also has tennis courts, a fitness center and a full-service spa to pamper and polish you.

Across from the hotel, at 15th Street and Camino Del Mar, is **Stratford Square**, an English Tudor-style building that is home to restaurants and other businesses. The building used to house the "Schwabs of Del Mar," a drug store and soda fountain where Hollywood stars hung out during racing season. Historians say it was "the" place to go, a sort of gossip central. It's said that Jennifer Jones ordered thick, syrupy sundaes topped with lots of whipped cream. Rita Hayworth liked vanilla; Buddy Abbott, chocolate.

A few steps from Stratford Square is **Sbicca**, an American bistro serving creative cuisine. From there, it's a short walk to **Seagrove Park**, where you can sit on benches overlooking the beach. Cross the railroad tracks that run along the coast and you'll come to Powerhouse Park, a grassy expanse where locals and tourists alike spread picnic blankets, play Frisbee, or listen to concerts on summer nights. The park is anchored by the restored Powerhouse, a community center where residents gather for everything from lectures to T'ai Chi. Next door, for dining by the sea, are **Jake's Del Mar** and the **Poseidon** restaurants. There's no ocean view at **Pamplemousse Grille**–up the road on Via de la Valle–but no matter. With food this fabulous, you won't miss it! Chef Jeffrey Strauss serves eclectic French fare from lobster ravioli to mixed grill of game (save room for the pear tarte Tatin). This elegant restaurant, across from the Del Mar Race Track, is a real winner.

To reach Del Mar, exit I-5 at Del Mar Heights Road or Via de la Valle and head west toward the ocean.

Del Mar Race Track

Del Mar has long been an escape for Angelenos in the summertime. Hollywood stars flocked here in the 30s and 40s to bask on the beach and play the horses at the Del Mar Race Track. The track, as the song says, is "where the turf meets the surf"–just furlongs from the Pacific Ocean. Crooner Bing Crosby not only sang the song, he founded the track in 1937. For this venture Crosby, who bred horses in nearby Rancho Santa Fe, teamed up with actor Pat O'Brien and other Hollywood pals, including Oliver "Babe" Hardy, who was said to have been a big horseplayer.

But until Crosby and O'Brien borrowed on their life insurance and ponied up $400,000, the track was in danger of being side-tracked. Opening day was July 3, 1937, a gala event that drew 15,000 spectators and stars like Barbara Stanwyck and Robert Taylor. Crosby and O'Brien personally greeted fans as they passed through the gate. Douglas Fairbanks Sr. and his new wife, Lady Ashley, helped Bing celebrate the victory of his

The Coaster, Del Mar

San Diego Polo Club

The Inn at Rancho Santa Fe

horse, High Strike, in the very first race at Del Mar.

Opening Day at Del Mar has been a tradition ever since. Women wear chic chapeaus to watch the races from the members-only Turf Club. There's even an annual competition called "The One and Only Truly Fabulous Hats Contest" to determine which hats are the "top hats" in different categories, from glamorous to outrageous. The judges are always amazed at what can be glued, stacked, built or balanced on one's head. It's hard to say which is more entertaining–watching the horses–or the people. Spectators can also sit in the stands, or pack picnics and watch all the action from the infield.

Bing himself would probably be surprised at how this little track by the sea has grown. It is now considered one of America's premier racetracks with about a half billion dollars bet on the horses each summer at Del Mar and its southern California satellites.

The racing season at Del Mar runs from late July through mid-September.

Balloon Rides

Perhaps the best way to see the North County is by air. Hot air balloon, that is. At $125 to $160 per person, depending on the season, it's not cheap, but it will definitely lift your spirits. You'll feel like Dorothy in the *Wizard of Oz* when you step into the basket. And once aloft, floating high above town and country, you'll know you aren't in Kansas anymore. Up here, the peace and quiet are broken only by the chatter of birds, and a gentle SWOOOSSSHHH as hot air fills the balloon.

Far from the bustling freeways and madding crowds, you get a sense of solitude and serenity. And it's fun to see those multi-million dollar Rancho Santa Fe mansions from the air–your guide will point out just *who* lives *where*. The landing can be a bit bumpy, but then, this is no MD-11. Spotters who follow your flight path from the ground pick you up. Back on earth, your balloon pilot will toast you with champagne and hors d'oeuvres and commemorate your flight with a certificate and pin. The one-hour flights are at sunrise and sunset. But the entire experience takes about three hours, including check-in, travel to the launch site in a van, inflation, and pick up. The baskets hold four to 12 passengers, so unless you've got a big family, you'll be sharing the gondola with strangers. But you won't be strangers for long. There's something about being crowded together in a balloon that makes people bond.

Legoland

Farther north, in Carlsbad, you'll find San Diego's newest amusement park, Legoland California. Billed as a land without limits, it’s a country just for kids (kids from three to 12, that is–older kids may find it too tame). Lego comes from the Danish, "leg godt:" literally, "play well." The park offers more than 40 exhibits and rides, with lots of hands-on fun. It may lack the bells and whistles of mega parks like Disneyland, but it offers magic on a much smaller scale, quite literally.

The park's centerpiece is *Miniland USA*, an engineering marvel all in miniature, made out of 20 million Lego bricks. For its creators, this was definitely *not* child's play! Five geographical areas, including New York City, San Francisco and Washington D.C., have been painstakingly built down to the most miniscule detail–diminutive window washers hang from skyscrapers, teeny skaters take to the "ice" in Rockefeller Center. Even the trees are tiny. Bonsais and other pint-sized plants are tended by full-time (and full-sized) gardeners. This minute metropolis is also interactive. Push a button at the New Orleans exhibit, for example, and a Lego band plays. Miniland's fascination for both young and old is definitely in the details.

You can also hop on the Dragon Coaster in *Castle Hill*, or pretend you're a knight on a charger at the *Royal Joust*. Then pause for some medieval merriment in the *Courtyard Theatre* where jesters entertain little lords and ladies. Your kids can pan for "precious" stones at the *King's Treasure* or climb nets and slide down wooden chutes in *The Hideaways*. My son was engrossed listening to his echo in the "witching well," or pretending to be a "castle convict," behind bars in a medieval cart.

Kids can navigate the Legoland waters at *Skipper School* or put the pedal to the metal at *Driving School* (no tailgating–or adults–allowed.) There are also the *Flight Squadron* and *Sky Patrol* rides, and a Rube Goldberg-style contraption called the *Sky Cycle*, billed as a "people-powered pedal car." For a bird's-eye view of the park and Pacific Ocean, try the *Kid Power Towers*, a self-propelled ride up to the top, with a free-fall down.

Prepare to get wet at the *Water Works*! (After several visits, I finally learned to pack an extra set of clothes.) Kids can squirt Lego animals–and each other–with giant squirt guns, or trigger jets of water with the touch of their feet. They can even strike up the band by stepping on sensors embedded in the pavement.

Little kids will especially like *Fairy Tale Brook*, a gentle boat tour that meanders by the three little Lego pigs and other characters, and *Safari Trek*, a jeep tour that winds through the "wild"–past life-size zebras, giraffes, ostriches and other animals all made from those ubiquitous little bricks.

But perhaps the best part of Legoland is hands *on*. You'll never hear anyone say, "don't touch!" in the *Imagination Zone*. Here, kids can build fanciful structures, speedy race-cars, or computerized robots. And in the *Maniac Challenge*, children learn by doing, using Lego computer software and interface programs.

Legoland is not for older kids looking for thrills. The rides here are pink–not white–knuckle, and for good reason. But Lego's focus on its core market, families with young children, has given it a niche–at least until all those little kids grow up.

To reach Legoland, exit I-5 at Cannon Road and head east.

Carlsbad

Practically next door to Legoland is the **Grand Pacific Palisades Resort & Hotel**, 12.5 acres on a ridge overlooking the ocean and the famous **Flower Fields of Carlsbad Ranch**. The resort's palm-filled lobby leads to an Olympic-sized pool with Pacific views. The resort also has spas, a fitness center with sauna, clubroom and game room. For bratwurst and a brew, try the resort's on-site restaurant, **Karl Strauss Brewery & Grill**.

The Flower Fields are a local landmark–row upon row of ranunculi stretching as far as the eye can see. Every spring, about 200,000 visitors flock to these fields striped in broad bands of vibrant color: white, gold, red, fuchsia, orange and pink.

Just around the corner are the Carlsbad Company Stores, an upscale outlet mall with scores of stores including Barneys New York, Bose, Calvin Klein, Cole-Haan, Donna Karan, Ellen Tracy, GAP, Polo Ralph Lauren, and many more. For a break after all that shopping, there's **Bellefleur Winery & Restaurant**, **Ruby's Diner**, **Starbucks Coffee** and other spots.

To find the Grand Pacific, Flower Fields, and Carlsbad Company Stores take the Palomar Airport Road exit from I-5 and head east.

Legoland, New York City

Legoland, Central Park

Near Carlsbad, perched on a hilltop above the Pacific is the **Four Seasons Resort Aviara**. This world-class resort, set on 200 acres, is surrounded by gardens, a championship golf course designed by Arnold Palmer, and private residences in the master planned Aviara community. The resort's low-rise buildings are Spanish-Colonial in style, housing guest rooms and suites that open onto private balconies or landscaped terraces.

The lobby has gleaming marble floors and a large picture window overlooking the Batiquitos Lagoon, a sanctuary for native wildlife. You can have afternoon tea or an evening cocktail in the elegant **Lobby Lounge**, with its marble bar, baby grand, and tasteful decorations in tones of taupe and rich wood. It opens onto the **Lounge Terrace** with ocean views. The **California Bistro** serves California-style cuisine in a comfortable setting, inside or outside. And the award-winning **Vivace** serves Tuscan dishes, featuring fresh seafood and seasonal ingredients. The restaurant is both elegant and warm, with a Roman stone fireplace, faux-finished Venetian walls, wood paneling and stone floors. There's informal dining at the **Ocean Pool Bar & Gril**l. After a round of golf, you can relax in the **Clubhouse lounge** or the **Argyle** restaurant with its view of the 18th green.

The Four Seasons' golf course has been rated among the top new resort courses in the country by golfing magazines. Facilities include a driving range and putting and pitching greens. There's also a pool, tennis complex with six courts, a spa and fitness center. Unwind with steam, sauna, and beauty treatments. Or get a makeover at the Jose Eber Salon, which offers hair services, manicures and pedicures, and make-up.

Your children need a vacation, too. *The Kids For All Seasons* program keeps them busy and gives parents a break–time to explore this beautiful bluff-top resort, the **Batiquitos Lagoon**, or the seaside town of Carlsbad.

To reach The Four Seasons Resort Aviara at 7100 Four Seasons Point, take the Poinsettia exit off I-5 and head east.

Close by is **La Costa Resort and Spa**, best known for its two PGA championship golf courses. In keeping with the golf theme, even the bellhops wear knickers. The resort has been home for 30 years to the Tournament of Champions, the competition exclusively for winners of PGA Tour events. It now hosts World Golf Championships—Accenture Match Play Championship. The La Costa Golf School will help you polish your game. The Spa at La Costa—renovated at a cost of $12 million—offers everything from massage to body wraps, Roman waterfalls to whirlpools. The La Costa Racquet Club offers 21 courts and a tennis school. And there's Camp La Costa for the kids.

At **Legends California Bistro**, guests can dine indoors or out, overlooking the lush green fairways and rolling hills. **BlueFire Grill** serves coastal delacacies amid cascading fountains and crackling fire-pits.

La Costa Resort and Spa is on Costa del Mar Road in Carlsbad. From I-5, take the La Costa Avenue exit.

"The Guardian of the Waters"

Tuna Park

"The Cabrillo," Coronado Ferry

California Tower, Balboa Park

Opposite: An aerial of Balboa Park

Shelter Island

Petco Park, new home of the Padres'

Mission Beach and Mission Bay

Windsurfing Mission Bay

"Giant Dipper" roller coaster, Belmont Park

SeaWorld orcas

Friendly dolphin at SeaWorld

Electric Fountain at night, Broadway

San Diego Museum of Art, Balboa Park

Opposite: The North County Mormon Temple at night

Library, University of California San Diego

Victorian houses at Heritage Park, Old Town

Jesse Shepherd House, "Villa Montezuma," 1887

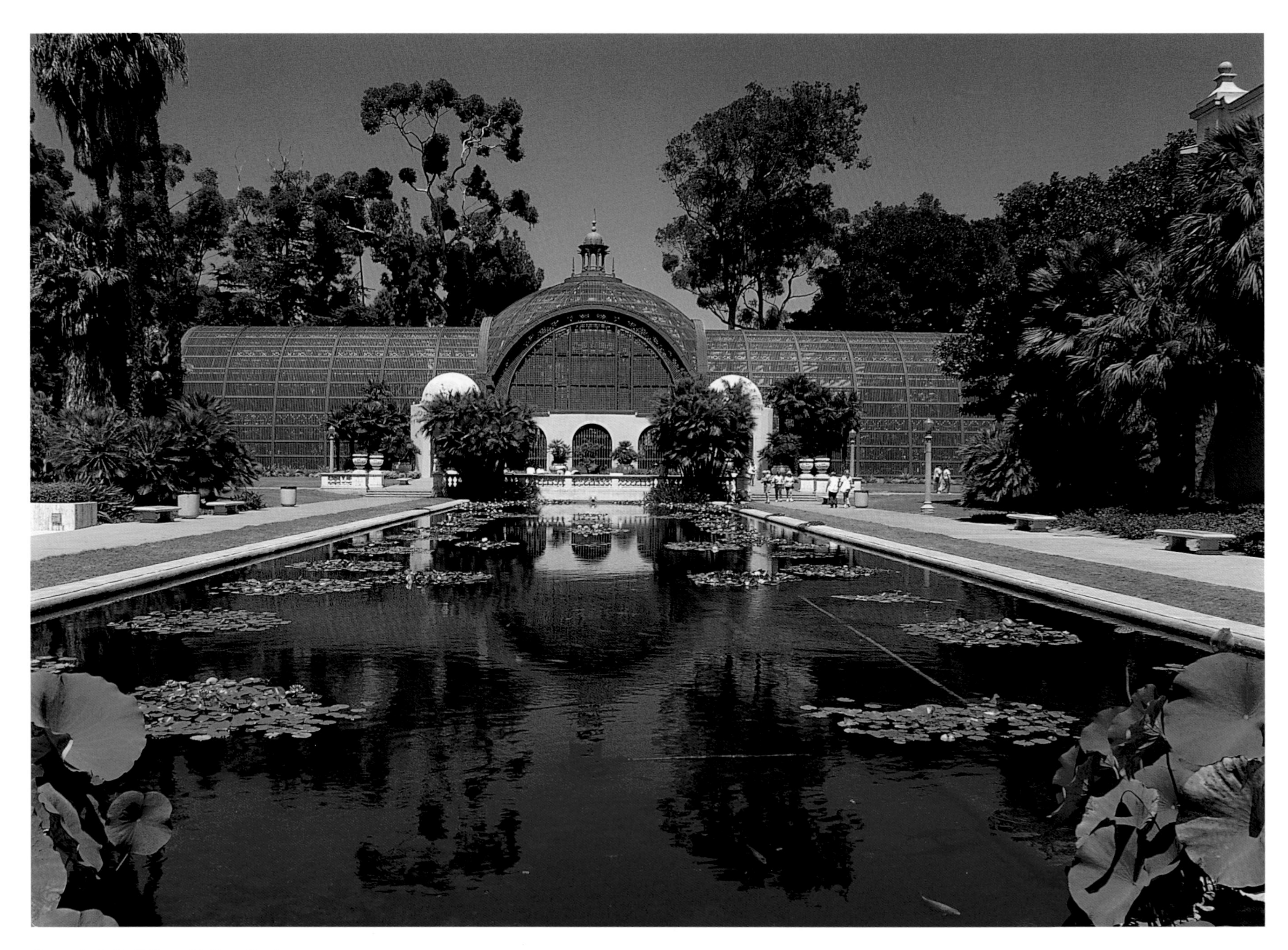

Botanical Building, Balboa Park

Ranunculus gardens, Carlsbad

Rancho Santa Fe

This is where the other half lives–Rancho Santa Fe–"The Ranch" to people lucky enough to call it home. You reach it along winding country roads lined with white fences, groves of willow and eucalyptus trees, sprawling ranches, equestrian centers and stables. Children ride horses or play soccer on Saturday mornings; adults play polo on Sunday afternoons at the San Diego Polo Club.

Rancho Santa Fe village is charming, with its Spanish Colonial Revival architecture, white stucco and red tile roofs. Even the hunter green signs are tasteful. There are some boutiques and antique stores for browsing on Paseo Delicias, the village's main street. But Rancho Santa Fe is short on shops and long on banks and real estate offices. It's easy to see why. The median price of a home here is 2.25 million dollars. That's *median*. *The Robb Report* rated this exclusive enclave the top affluent community in the country, edging out Greenwich, Palm Beach, and other pricey places. One perk of buying in the Ranch–you also get membership in the Rancho Santa Fe Golf Club.

Rancho Santa Fe is also rich in history. According to the Rancho Santa Fe Historical Society, it began as Rancho San Dieguito when Juan Maria Osuna was awarded a land grant of nearly 9,000 acres in 1845. Osuna was a former soldier who became Mayor of the Pueblo of San Diego. In 1906, the Santa Fe Railroad bought the land, and planted thousands of eucalyptus trees for railroad ties. As it turned out, the wood wouldn't hold the spikes! That was fortunate for the Ranch, because eucalyptus trees flourish there to this day, along with citrus groves.

In the 1920's, Rancho Santa Fe became one of California's first planned communities, according to the Historical Society. It was tied together by a single architectural theme, the Spanish Colonial Revival. Lilian Rice, one of the state's first woman architects, oversaw the project and designed many of the commercial buildings as well as a school, homes and row houses. She also rehabilitated two adobe houses that once belonged to the Osuna family. Bing Crosby bought one of them in 1932, and Rice designed an addition. It's a tribute to her work that Rancho Santa Fe was designated a California State Historic Landmark in 1989. Many of her buildings are also on the National Register of Historic Places.

The first building in Rancho Santa Fe was La Morada at the western end of Paseo Delicias. It's now **The Inn at Rancho Santa Fe**. The Santa Fe Land Improvement Company asked Rice to design a guesthouse as a sort of sales promotion--a place to put up prospective buyers. The main building was built of adobe blocks made right on the site. Even though it has changed hands several times–and even its name in 1941–The Inn remains the focus of the village. It is now run by a third generation of hoteliers who believe each guest is an individual–and should be treated that way. Most of the inn's guest rooms are in cottages, many with private patios, wet bars and fireplaces. The living room, which has comfortable furniture and a fireplace, is decorated with Chinese paintings, Oriental rugs, and model ships. The inn's restaurant has an outdoor patio and a cozy library lined with books and lit by firelight. The Inn also has tennis, croquet, a heated pool, and its own cottage on the beach in Del Mar. And guests can use two private courses, including the Rancho Santa Fe Golf Club, less than a mile away. The Inn is on 20 acres of landscaped grounds and gardens in the shade of the towering eucalyptus trees that figure so prominently in the history of Rancho Santa Fe.

According to the Historical Society, Lilian Rice also designed three buildings, each with its own facade, that formed the first block of the village on Paseo Delicias. The cornerstone is a stucco building with recessed windows and red clay tile at the corner of Paseo Delicias and Avenida de Acacias. It housed offices for the Santa Fe Land Improvement Company. The Francisco Building, with its arched doorway and quatrefoil, was the local headquarters for the land company and, much later, became Ashley's, the Ranch's only market. The Country Squire Courtyard, with its distinctive arches, now houses a tree-shaded patio, shops, and the acclaimed **Mille Fleurs** restaurant, rated among the top restaurants in the country. The restaurant's chef, Chef Martin Woesle, blends classic French dishes with California cuisine. Bertrand Hug is the amiable proprietor.

The restaurant credits nearby Chino's farm for produce that has attained a national reputation. Other restaurants–Alice Water's Chez Panisse in Berkeley and Wolfgang Puck's Spago in Los Angeles to name just two–feature Chino's products on their menus. On Saturday morning, Chino's looks like a luxury car lot, as well-heeled customers line up for perfect produce and herbs. You can even listen to classical music as you squeeze the tomatoes. Join the crowd, but get there early.

A few miles away is the **Rancho Valencia Resort**, a haven for the tennis power set, with 18 courts, a renowned tennis clinic, and pros to polish your game. There's even a very proper croquet lawn if you're feeling genteel.

Rancho Valencia is set on 40 acres of manicured grounds dotted with orange groves. The architecture is reminiscent of early California haciendas. In the main building, a Mexican-tiled courtyard features a fountain, fireplace, and terra cotta pots brimming with bougainvillea. It leads to the reception area, restaurant, and terrace overlooking the tennis courts.

Stay in intimate casitas, with custom furnishings, fireplaces, wet bars and private patios. Or for the ultimate vacation, the Hacienda is complete with three bedrooms, kitchen and living room, its own private pool, Jacuzzi and cabana. (Just don't ask how much!) Rancho Valencia also has pools, a fitness center and spa treatments (try a massage to soothe that tennis elbow). Linger in the lovely restaurant, called simply, the **Dining Room**. It is both rustic and romantic, casual yet elegant, with its high-beamed ceiling, fireplace, and fine cuisine. You can also dine outside in the courtyard, weather permitting.

Rancho Valencia is located at 5921 Valencia Circle in Rancho Santa Fe.

A visiting tall ship from Indonesia

Opposite: Sailing in San Diego Bay

US
67745
IMPERIAL BANK
IMPERIAL
San Diego
Bank

San Diego Wild Animal Park

The San Diego Wild Animal Park is a sprawling 1,800-acre wildlife sanctuary where animals roam free in settings designed to recreate their native homelands. It is about 30 miles north of downtown San Diego in the San Pasqual Valley near Escondido. Here you'll find 3,200 rare and endangered animals. The park is also a lush botanical garden abloom with more than 3,500 species of exotic plants.

A good way to see it all is via the *Wgasa Bush Line Railway*, a 55-minute safari-by-rail. Guides describe the animals you see, as well as their habitats–African and Asian plains and prairies carved from the mesas and canyons. On a trip one spring, we saw baby animals just after birth, their mothers shielding them protectively as we passed.

If you'd rather hoof it, the *Heart of Africa* exhibit takes you on a walking safari through a 32-acre African wilderness. You'll see a range of habitats–forest, savanna and wetlands. There are hundreds of animals here from cheetahs to colobus monkeys, warthogs to wattled cranes. And you can even feed giraffes by hand. "It's as close as you can get to Africa," says a park brochure, "without having to swat away tsetse flies."

Or you can go on a photo caravan, if you book ahead. An open-air truck will take you inside the preserve, giving you a look that's up close and personal. You're sure to get a good shot–not to mention, experience–as rhinos lumber alongside your truck. You might have to remind yourself this is San Diego–not the Serengeti.

Condor Ridge is a habitat for North American animals, and home to endangered species such as the California condor. This is the first time the park has given visitors a look at these nearly extinct birds. In fact, nearly half the condors still flying today were hatched at the park as part of the California Condor Recovery Project.

Nairobi Village has animals, exhibits, restaurants, shops and picnic areas. There are also daily shows and demonstrations. Kids love *Lorikeet Landing*, where they can feed the birds; and the *Petting Kraal*, where gentle gazelle, antelope and deer pose patiently for pictures.

The park has a number of animal shows, including free-flying birds. They'll amaze you not only with their aerial agility, but also with their singing ability. Pancho the parrot has "I Left My Heart in San Francisco" down pat.

And there's plenty of flora, literally millions of plants, in the park's exotic gardens. At the *Kupanda Falls Botanical Center* you can take a 1.25 mile walk through a variety of gardens, Baja, native plant, and bonsai among them.

If you just can't get enough of the park during the day, try it at night. During the summer months you can experience the *Park at Dark*, or you can even stay all night at a *Roar & Snore* camp over, complete with tales (tall, no doubt) around a campfire. Listening to animal sounds just may lull you to sleep.

The San Diego Wild Animal Park is the sister facility to the "World Famous San Diego Zoo," owned and operated by the non-profit Zoological Society of San Diego.

To reach the San Diego Wild Animal Park from I-5, take the Via Rancho Parkway exit and follow the signs six miles east.

Day Trips

Julian

Julian is nestled in San Diego's backcountry at an elevation of 4,200 feet. A visit here is like stepping back in time to small-town America. Many of the buildings lining historic Main Street date to the early 1900s. You can still get a malt at the Julian Drug Store/Miner's Diner with its old-fashioned marble-topped soda fountain. There's even a country store.

Julian used to be a gold rush town. Now the rush is for apples. Every fall, hordes of "lowlanders" invade this tiny town of 350 to poke around the shops and line up for thick pieces of apple pie. All this occurs during Julian Apple Days, the harvest season that runs from mid-September to mid-November. Tens of thousands of pies are sold during those months alone.

For Southern Californians, a trip to Julian is about as close as it gets to a change of season. So when the weather is as crisp as an apple and leaves crunch under foot, visitors come for a taste of autumn, as well as pie. San Diegans also flock here during the winter to play in the snow, something they don't often see at home.

Julian has tree-lined country lanes, grazing cattle, orchards and meadows. It's close to **Cuyamaca Rancho State Park** and the **Cleveland National Forest**, favorites for hiking and camping. When you're out that way don't forget to stop at the family-run **Dudley's Bakery** for the house specialty, raisin date nut bread, hot from the oven. And at **Manzanita Ranch**, you can pick up fruit, cider and pumpkins.

To reach Julian, take Highway 78 east through Escondido, Ramona, and Santa Ysabel.

Temecula

The wine country of Temecula Valley is about an hour's drive from San Diego north along Interstate 15 past rocky mountains and rows of citrus and avocado groves. Exit at Rancho California Road, and head east. At first, you'll pass so many spanking new developments, you'll wonder how there could be room for wineries. But just four miles from the I-15 exit, you'll see row upon row of grapes stepped on the hillside.

This area was discovered in the 1840s by wine great Jean Louis Vignes and rediscovered in the 1960s by growers and wine experts. It is a choice site for wine-growing, with a climate similar to the fine wine regions of southern France. Cool Pacific breezes flow through a gap in the coastal range, creating the long growing season needed for premium varietal grapes. Growers boast "the perfect balance" of geography, climate and soil "is found nowhere else."

Stop first at the **Thornton Winery**, with its Mediterranean-style manor house, for tours and tasting. Here you can learn how sparkling wine is produced, a method pioneered by French monk Dom Perignon 300 years ago.

The winery's **Cafe Champagne** provides Tuscan-style vineyard ambiance. Dine inside, or outside on a terrace cooled by ceiling fans with a fountain splashing nearby. The **Champagne Lounge** opens daily at 11 a.m. for tasting. On weekends, the winery offers tours and live jazz concerts from spring to fall. There's also a gift shop and herb garden, where the chef picks fresh herbs for the daily specials. Thornton Winery is located at 32575 Rancho California Road.

Bengal tiger, San Diego Wild Animal Park

Opposite: Quail Botanical Gardens, Encinitas

There are more than a dozen wineries in the valley, ranging from large operations to small, family-run establishments. Many offer tours, tasting, and picnic tables overlooking the vineyards. All you need is a bottle of wine, a loaf of bread, and thou (don't forget the cheese).

If you want to make a weekend of it, there are a half dozen hostelries, including the **Temecula Creek Inn**, with 80 rooms and a 27-hole championship golf course in a rustic setting. The inn's **Temet Grill Restaurant** serves Wine Country cuisine. The Temecula Creek Inn is at 44501 Rainbow Canyon Road.

Before you leave the valley, visit **Old Town Temecula**, preserved in the architectural style of the 1890s, with its gift and antique shops, museum and visitor's center, and restaurants. And for a bird's-eye view, take a balloon flight over the wine country.

To reach Temecula from San Diego, take Interstate 15 north and exit at Indio/Highway 79.

Anza-Borrego Desert State Park

To reach this huge state reserve, drive east from Julian to the little town of Borrego Springs. The scenery will justify the long drive, especially in the springtime. Anyone who thinks the desert is dry and colorless hasn't been to Anza-Borrego in this season. For a few weeks every spring the normally abstemious plants that blanket East County's hills and mesas blossom forth suddenly in a spendthrift display of color, a riot of oranges, reds, and yellows.

When Anza-Borrego is in bloom, thousands of pilgrims arrive to witness this rite of spring. In fact, on weekends the desert can get downright congested with cars and tour buses. So if you have a choice, visit the park during the week. But in any case, don't miss it. The Park's Wildflower Hotline (760-767-4684) will tell you what's abloom.

From Borrego Springs, follow the signs to Anza-Borrego itself. A good place to start your tour is the visitor's center, which has a museum and garden where you can take a crash course in the desert ecology.

Not far from the center are walking trails that should satisfy all but the most ambitious hikers. One of the most popular, the Palm Canyon Trail, follows a clear, spring-fed stream that winds out of the mountains to water the desert below. As you walk onward (and upward) you'll experience a remarkably varied terrain filled with flowering ocotillo, agave, and a host of other desert plants and cacti. If you keep a sharp eye out, you may even catch a glimpse of the bighorn sheep that range in these parts.

A few miles up the trail is Palm Canyon, one of the last refuges for California's only native palm tree. This pleasant little oasis offers shady relief from the rigors of the trail. Here hikers can picnic beneath the trees, cool themselves in a waterfall that spills out of the rocks, or simply relax in preparation for the return trek.

To reach Anza-Borrego, take route 78 east and head north on S3 to the town of Borrego Springs. From there follow the signs to the park.

Palomar Observatory

Another attraction in northeast San Diego County is the Palomar Observatory, which is open every day of the year except December 24th and 25th. Owned and operated by Pasadena's Caltech, Palomar has been a working research facility since 1948. Visitors are welcome, as long as they don't make nuisances of themselves. The observatory gift shop is open year round on weekends and daily in July and August. Visitors can also take a self-guided tour and view the impressive 200-inch Hale Telescope from a gallery in the dome. From downtown San Diego, Palomar is about two hours by car, but the mountain vistas and scenery alone are ample recompense for the time and gasoline.

To reach the observatory, take California 76 to S6 and follow the signs to the top of Palomar Mountain.

Del Mar hot air balloon rides

Palomar Observatory

Anza-Borrego Desert State Park

Tijuana & Baja California

Just a half hour from downtown San Diego lies *La Linea*, the border between the United States and Mexico, the busiest crossing in the world. Drive across the border at **San Ysidro**, and spend a day browsing in **Tijuana**. Or head for the beaches of Baja, along a scenic coastal road. But unless you relish a long wait at the border on your return trip from Tijuana, take the San Diego Trolley (cars are marked "Blue Line San Ysidro"), or walk. You can leave your car at the many parking lots off Interstate 805 just before the border. (One is located next to the **San Diego Factory Outlet Center**, where you can find great buys on merchandise from Mikasa, Izod/Gant, Bass Shoes, Levi's, Maidenform, Nike, and many other manufacturers.) From there, it's a short walk into Tijuana, or a quick shuttle ride. Head for ***Avenida Revolucion***, perhaps the best place to see (and taste) Tijuana. Here you'll find eight blocks of restaurants, nightspots, and shops filled with Mexican arts and crafts, and leather goods. The **Fronton Palacio**, between Seventh and Eighth streets, offers a look at the world's fastest game, jai-lai, and you can wager, too.

If you take a taxi or car, drive to the ***Zona del Rio*** (River Zone), where you'll find more restaurants and nightspots to choose from along ***Avenida Paseo de los Heroes***. The city's cultural center is also located here, with its wraparound theatre, art exhibits, and bookstore. Just south of *Paseo de los Heroes* is ***Agua Caliente Boulevard*** where you'll find the bullring and racetrack. **The Caliente Racetrack** has both thoroughbred and greyhound racing, and pari-mutuel betting.

About 45 minutes from the border is **Rosarito Beach**, where you can bargain at the roadside stands or sip a margarita at the **Rosarito Beach Hotel**. At the **Festival Plaza** nearby, there's a hotel, restaurants and bars, shops and special events. Fifteen minutes farther, and you'll come to **Puerto Nuevo**, where lobster is the local specialty at the many restaurants. Back on the highway toward **Ensenada**, stop in at **La Fonda's**, a roadside restaurant and inn. Dine on the outdoor terrace framed by bougainvillea with a view of the broad sweep of beach below. Ensenada is an hour or so beyond, at the end of a winding road that yields breathtaking views of the rocky coastline. The city bustles with activity. There are lots of shops to browse, many offering high-quality Mexican handicrafts. Stop in at **Hussong's**, a favorite bar among American tourists. And have a fish taco at the line of stands across from the fish market while you watch the fishmongers feed greedy pelicans.

If you drive your own car across the border, be sure to buy Mexican car insurance. If you're driving a rental car, check with the rental agency. Many prohibit taking their cars across the border.

About the Author

Andrea Naversen is a veteran newscaster, network television correspondent, newspaper reporter, magazine editor and author.

She has served as an anchor and reporter at San Diego television stations XETV Fox 6 News, KFMB-TV and KUSI-TV, where she has covered the city's life and times for nearly two decades.

Before moving to San Diego, Andrea lived in New York and Los Angeles, working as a network correspondent for CBS News and ABC News. Her assignments for national news shows including *The CBS Evening News*, *The CBS Morning News*, *Sunday Morning*, *ABC's Good Morning America*, *World News Tonight*, and *Nightline* took her all over the United States, Europe, and the Middle East. She also anchored ABC's Newsbrief and Business Brief on the West Coast, and was a substitute anchor on ABC's *World News This Morning* in Washington D.C.

Andrea graduated cum laude from Miami University in Ohio with a Bachelor of Arts degree in English. She began her journalism career as a reporter for *The Plain Dealer*, Ohio's largest daily newspaper, covering everything from politics to the police beat. After freelancing for *Time* and *Business Week* magazines, she became associate editor of *Pittsburgher* magazine. Andrea's first television job was at WTAE-TV in Pittsburgh where she served as a general assignment reporter and headed the station's consumer investigative team.

Andrea, the mother of a young boy, is an active and effective advocate for children's causes. She conceived, as well as co-chaired, *Hats Off to Children*, a fundraiser that has netted hundreds of thousands of dollars to benefit Children's Hospital and Health Center, and she is on the National Board for Kids Korps USA.

Andrea lives in Rancho Santa Fe with her husband, a former commercial airline pilot, and their son, Tyler.

About the Photographer

Kenneth Naversen–Andrea's older brother–is a freelance photographer who specializes in architectural and travel subjects. He is a recipient of an Art Critics Fellowship from the National Endowment for the Arts and holds a master's degree in Art and Photography. His work has appeared in numerous books and magazines. He is the author as well as the photographer of several Beautiful America titles including *California Victorians*.

Mission San Luis Rey de Francia, Oceanside

Back cover: The "Star of India" under full sail